Published by Grolier Books, a division of Grolier
Enterprises Inc.

Disney Presents The Wonderful World of Knowledge
ISBN 0-7172-8929-X
Human Body ISBN 0-7172-8932-X

© 1999 Disney

First published in 1999

Printed and bound in China by
Toppan Printing Company

Originated in Italy by Articolor

Designed and compiled by
Marshall Editions Developments Limited

GROLIER
BOOKS

PRESENTS
The Wonderful World of Knowledge

HUMAN BODY

Using The Wonderful World of Knowledge

Mickey, Minnie, Donald, Daisy, Goofy, and Pluto are ready to take you on an adventure ride through the world of learning. Discover the secrets of science, nature, our world, the past, and much more. Climb aboard and enjoy the ride.

Look here for a general summary of the theme

Labels tell you what's happening in the pictures

Mickey's ears lead you to one of the main topics

The pictures by themselves can tell you a lot, even before you read a word

Watch out for special pages where Mickey takes a close look at some key ideas

The Solar System

☞**T**he Solar System is the [name] given to our Sun and its family [of] planets. It also includes the [many] moons, millions of pieces of [rock] called asteroids and meteor[s], and frozen lumps of dust an[d ice] called comets. Everything els[e we] can see in the sky is outside [the] Solar System and is far, far away. Every single star is itself a sun, and each may have its own family of planets and moons.

Saturn is surrounded by beautiful rings

REPTILES AND AMPHIBIANS

False-eyed frog

Color and Camouflage

Frogs and toads come in nearly every imaginable color, even gold or black. They have a wide range of patterns, from spots and stripes to zigzags.

Color and pattern help frogs and toads survive. Bright colors warn that they may be poisonous. Drab colors camouflage them, or hide them against their background. Many tree frogs are exactly the same green as leaves, while others look like bark. The Asian horned toad has the best camouflage of all. Folds of patchy, brown skin and a flat body make it look like a dead leaf when it lies still on the forest floor.

Markings look like eyes

For extra protection, bad-smelling liquid oozes out around false eyes

FALSE-EYED FROG
The South American false-eyed frog has large markings on its flanks that look like eyes. These fool some predators into thinking that they are looking at a much larger animal, such as a cat or bird.

Folds of brown skin give perfect camouflage

Flat body is hard to see among dead leaves

Asian horned toad

Dog sniffing curiously at the toad

COLOR AND CAMOUFLAGE

Strawberry arrow frog

POISON-DART FROGS
Deadly poison oozes from the skin of Central and South American poison-dart frogs. People in the rain forest rub the tips of their arrows and blowpipe darts on the skin of these frogs to collect the poison to use for hunting.

Blue poison-dart frog

Oriental fire-bellied toad defending itself against a dog

Skin oozes a stinging fluid

Bright colored belly

Green and black back

FIRE-BELLIED TOAD
When cornered by a predator, the Oriental fire-bellied toad of eastern Asia arches its back and rears up on its legs to show its fiery underside. Wise attackers back off, because the toad's skin oozes a stinging, bad-tasting fluid.

Toad rears up on its back legs

FIND OUT MORE
MAMMALS: Camouflage
PLANET EARTH: Forests

16   17

Mickey's page numbers help you look things up. Don't forget there's a glossary and index at the back of each book

Goofy and his friends know how to give you a chuckle on every topic

Mickey points you to more information in other books in your *The Wonderful World of Knowledge*

FIND OUT MORE
MAMMALS: Camouflage
PLANET EARTH: Forests

AMAZING FACTS
★ The Sun is enormous compared to the planets. It is nearly 1,000 times more massive than the giant planet Jupiter.

Your favorite characters present some facts to astound you and your friends

AMAZING FACTS
★ The Sun is enormous compared to the planets. It is nearly 1,000 times more massive than the giant planet Jupiter.

THE SOLAR SYSTEM

HOW OUR SOLAR SYSTEM WAS FORMED

1 The Solar System formed 4.6 billion years ago. It started at the center of an enormous swirling cloud of gas and dust.

2 The Sun burst into flames and became a star. Its light and warmth spread throughout the new Solar System.

3 Gas and dust left over from making the Sun clumped together in places. These clumps grew bigger and formed the planets.

4 The planets closest to the Sun are small and made from rock and metal. The larger outer planets are made from gas and liquid.

Numbers lead *you step-by-step through how things happen*

Pluto is the farthest planet from the Sun

Each planet has its own path, or orbit   **Planet orbits**

Neptune is a cold, blue planet

ORBITING THE SUN
No matter how still you try to be, you are always moving. This is because the Earth – and all the other planets – are moving. They are flying through Space around the Sun in looping paths called orbits.

Colorful boxes *zoom in on information*

Uranus is tipped over on its side

THE "PULL" OF GRAVITY
If you throw a ball into the air, it comes down again. The invisible force that pulls it down to Earth is called gravity. The Earth's gravity holds us down on the ground. The Sun's gravity is strong enough to hold all its planets in their orbits.

Gravity pulls a ball to Earth

FIND OUT MORE
PLANET EARTH: Night and day
SCIENCE ALL AROUND US: Gravity

Mars is red and dusty   The Solar System

Mickey's helpers test some ideas themselves

Contents

Human Body

Built on a framework of bones, which are stronger than steel, is the most complicated of all machines – your body. It can breathe, smell, and taste. It can feel, talk, and walk. It eats, drinks, and thinks. It can even mend itself when it is damaged.

The brain is in charge, controlling all your body's systems. These work together throughout your life. As you grow up, your body will go through lots of changes, but if you look after your amazing body machine, it should last you for a long time.

Body Systems

The human body is made up of different systems, such as the nervous system and skeleton. While each system has its own special job, it works with other systems to keep the body alive and in perfect working order. Each system is a collection of organs. Each organ, such as the brain or stomach, has its own special job.

Circulatory system

Heart

Arteries (red) *carry blood away from the heart*

Veins (blue) *take blood to the heart*

Skull

SKELETON
The body is supported by a framework of bones called the skeleton. It protects the body's internal organs and provides an anchor for the muscles.

Ribs

Backbone, *or spine*

Pelvis

MUSCULAR SYSTEM
All the body's movements, such as running and jumping, are produced by muscles. Most muscles work by pulling the bones of the skeleton to which they are attached.

Arm muscles *(biceps and triceps)*

Thigh *muscles (quadriceps)*

CIRCULATORY SYSTEM
The heart, blood, and a network of blood vessels make up the circulatory system. Pumped along by the heart, blood delivers oxygen and nutrients to the body and takes away waste products.

Skeleton

Muscular system

Nose

Mouth

Windpipe

Lungs

Respiratory
system

RESPIRATORY SYSTEM

The body needs energy to stay alive. Energy is released from food by combining it with oxygen. The respiratory system supplies the body with oxygen. When a breath is taken in through the nose or mouth, air containing oxygen is carried along the windpipe and into the lungs.

Mouth

Stomach

Small intestine
breaks down food

Large intestine
absorbs water

DIGESTIVE SYSTEM

Everything you eat and drink is broken down by the digestive system into simple substances called nutrients. These are carried by the blood to all parts of the body and used to give you energy and make you grow.

Digestive
system

Brain

Network
of nerves

Spinal cord

NERVOUS SYSTEM

All the body's activities, including walking, seeing, thinking, and speaking, are controlled by the nervous system. The brain is in charge of the nervous system. It receives messages and sends out instructions along the spinal cord and the network of nerves.

Nervous
system

FIND OUT MORE
MAMMALS: Humans
PLANT LIFE: Plant parts

The Body's Cells

Cells are the body's building blocks. It takes billions of these tiny living units to make just one body. Each cell contains the information needed to build and operate the human body. Although different types of cells have their own shape, size, and job, all share the same basic structure.

STRUCTURE OF A CELL

A living cell is made up of a thin outer membrane, or skin, that surrounds a watery gel called cytoplasm. All the other minute cell parts float in the cytoplasm. The control center of the cell is called the nucleus. The nucleus contains the information needed to keep a cell alive and working properly.

BUILDING BLOCKS

Every day the body makes billions of new cells by a process called cell division. Some new cells are needed to replace old, worn-out ones. Others make the body grow. Cell division takes place in three main stages.

1 **Before it divides** in two, a cell makes a copy of the information in its nucleus.

2 **As the cell divides,** its nucleus splits into two equal parts, followed by the cytoplasm.

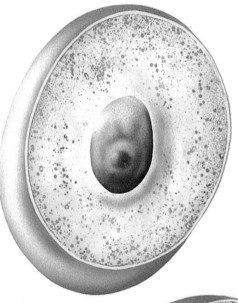

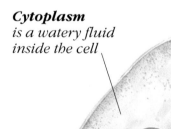

Cytoplasm *is a watery fluid inside the cell*

Cell membrane *is the outer boundary of the cell*

Nucleus controls *the workings of the cell*

Inside a cell

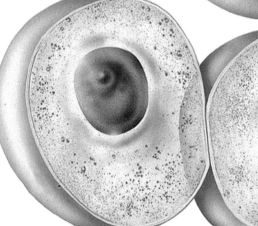

Dividing cell

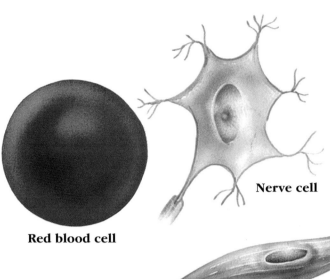

Red blood cell

Nerve cell

Liver cell

Skin cells

Muscle cell

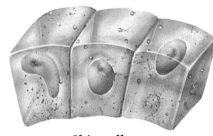

LOOKING AT CELLS

Each type of cell has its own shape and size, depending on what job it does. Cells are so tiny that you can only see them by using a microscope. A microscope magnifies the cells, or makes them look bigger, so that they and their parts can be seen by the human eye.

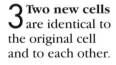

Cells can be studied under a microscope

3 **Two new cells** are identical to the original cell and to each other.

AMAZING FACTS

★ Bone marrow cells do not last very long – they divide just hours after they are made. But many nerve cells can last a whole lifetime.

> **FIND OUT MORE**
> **DINOSAURS:** Single-celled animals
> **GREAT INVENTIONS:** Microscope

Skin, Hair, Nails, and Teeth

The skin is the body's largest organ. It forms a barrier between the inside of the body and the outside world. It keeps out harmful germs, slows water loss, protects us from sunlight, enables us to feel, and helps to keep us warm. Both hair and nails grow from the skin. Teeth develop in the mouth. They are covered with a layer of hard enamel to help them crush food so it can be swallowed.

THE BODY'S OVERCOAT

Skin has two layers. The top layer, called the epidermis, protects the lower layer, called the dermis. The upper part of the epidermis is constantly being worn away and replaced by new cells. The epidermis also gives skin its color. The dermis contains hair roots and sweat glands, as well as nerve endings that enable us to feel heat, touch, and pain.

Hair keeps the head warm and protects it from strong sunlight

Skin is a stretchy, waterproof covering

Strong teeth break up food

Nails protect the tips of fingers and toes

Looking at skin, teeth, hair, and nails

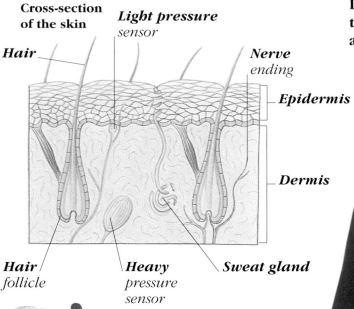

Cross-section of the skin

Hair

Light pressure sensor

Nerve ending

Epidermis

Dermis

Hair follicle

Heavy pressure sensor

Sweat gland

14

HAIRY HUMANS

Hair is made from keratin, a tough, waterproof substance. The cells in hair are dead. The only living part of a hair is its root. This is at the bottom of a pit in the skin called a follicle. Cells in the root divide and push upward so the hair grows.

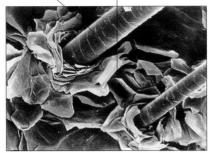

Hair   *Skin flakes*

Hairs growing out of follicles surrounded by skin flakes

TOUGH TEETH

Teeth cut and crush food. Roots anchor teeth in the jawbone. By the age of three, most children have 20 teeth, called baby teeth. From the age of six, new teeth, called permanent teeth, grow and replace the baby teeth. Adults usually have 32 permanent teeth.

AMAZING FACTS

★ No two people's fingerprints are exactly the same, not even those of identical twins.

★ Tooth enamel is the hardest substance in the body.

Crushing tooth   *Root*   *Cutting* tooth

Permanent teeth grow up through the gum

Cross-section of a child's jaw

Baby teeth are the first teeth

AT THE FINGERTIPS

Nails, like hair, are made of tough keratin. They protect our fingers and toes and help us to grip objects. Ridges on our fingertips also help us to grip. These ridges form patterns, called fingerprints, which are unique to each person.

FIND OUT MORE
BIRDS: Feathers
INSIDE MACHINES: Dentist's drill

The Skeleton

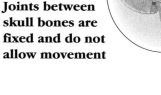

The adult skeleton is made up of 206 bones. It provides a strong, but light, framework that supports the body. Where bones meet, at joints, they move when pulled by muscles. This gives the body a wide range of movements. The skeleton also protects important parts of the body. The ribs shield the lungs and heart, and the skull protects the brain.

LITTLE AND LARGE

Bones come in many shapes and sizes. The strong, long bones in the legs enable the body to run and jump. The smaller bones in the hands help with tasks such as picking up and gripping things.

Joints between skull bones are fixed and do not allow movement

Shoulder blade (scapula)

Upper arm bone (humerus)

Hinge joint in the elbow allows the arm to straighten or bend

Ball-and-socket joint in the hip allows the leg to swivel in almost any direction

Ribs

Backbone

Pelvis

Thigh bone (femur)

Small lower leg bone (fibula)

Large lower leg bone (tibia)

Saddle joint in the thumb allows movement up, down, and sideways

Bones and joints in the body

AMAZING FACTS

★ The leg has only 4 bones; the foot has 26.

★ Living bone is six times stronger than a steel bar of the same weight.

Inner forearm *bone (ulna)*

Outer forearm *bone (radius)*

Spongy bone is found in the ends of long bones

Compact bone *is the hardest part of the bone*

Cross-section of a child's long bone

Spongy bone spaces filled with red bone marrow

INSIDE A BONE

The outer layer of a bone is made of a very hard material called compact bone. Inside is lighter spongy bone. Together they make the bone very strong but light. The spaces inside spongy bone contain red bone marrow. This makes millions of new blood cells every minute.

Knee cap *(patella)*

Vertebrae *make up the strong, flexible backbone*

JOINTS

Bones meet at joints. A few joints are stationary, but most are movable. An oily liquid, called synovial fluid, lies between the bones in a joint. This keeps the joint moving smoothly. Strong cords called ligaments hold the joint together.

STRONG SUPPORT

The backbone in babies is made up of 33 bones, called vertebrae. In adults, some join together so there are 24 vertebrae. The delicate spinal cord, which links the brain and nerves, lies protected inside the backbone.

Backbone

FIND OUT MORE
INSECTS AND SPIDERS: Exoskeleton
MAMMALS: Skeleton

Muscles and Movement

Muscles that move the body are called skeletal muscles. There are about 640 of them and they give the body its shape. Skeletal muscles are attached to bones. They work by contracting, or getting shorter. When a muscle contracts, it pulls the bone it is attached to. Skeletal muscles produce all movements, including running and chewing.

Facial muscles *allow us to make expressions*

Upper arm *muscles help us to lift or pull objects*

Upper body *muscles help us to bend and twist*

DIFFERENT SHAPES AND SIZES
Muscles vary in size and shape and are found all over the body. The longest are in the thigh. The biggest are the buttock muscles used in climbing and running. The tiniest muscles are inside the ear.

Thigh muscles *allow us to run and jump*

Using the muscles for movement

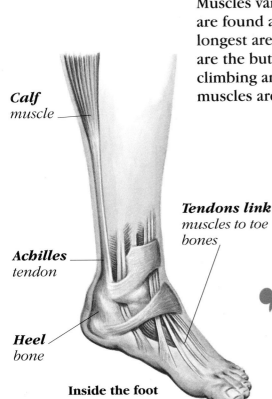

Calf *muscle*

Achilles *tendon*

Heel *bone*

Tendons link *muscles to toe bones*

Inside the foot

Group of four muscles *in the thigh, called the quadriceps, allow us to straighten our legs when we walk*

Muscle in the lower *leg helps us to bend our toes and feet*

TENDONS
Muscles are joined to bones by tough cords called tendons. When a muscle contracts, it pulls the tendon, which then pulls the bone. The Achilles tendon is a large tendon that joins the calf muscle to the heel bone.

MAKING A FACE

There are more than 40 small muscles in the face and neck. When they contract, they pull on the skin of the face to produce a wide range of facial expressions. These expressions, which include frowning and smiling, show whether a person is feeling sad, happy, angry, or frightened.

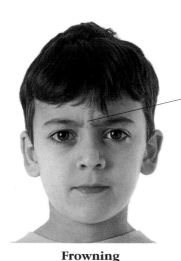

Corrugator *muscles in the forehead create a frown*

Risorius muscle *stretches the mouth to make a smile*

Frowning

Smiling

Triceps relaxes *and lengthens*

Triceps muscle *contracts and shortens to pull the forearm downward*

Biceps muscle *contracts and shortens to pull the forearm upward*

Biceps and triceps working together

Biceps *relaxes and lengthens*

MUSCLE PAIRS

Muscles usually work in pairs, with each muscle causing opposite movements. These are called antagonistic muscles. In the arm, the biceps muscle contracts and shortens to bend the arm at the elbow. The triceps contracts to straighten the arm.

AMAZING FACTS

★ Muscles make up nearly half the body's total weight.

★ Whether a person is asleep or awake, muscles move the eyes 100,000 times every day.

FIND OUT MORE
SCIENCE ALL AROUND US: Motion
SPORT: Gymnasts

19

The Lungs

To stay alive, the body needs oxygen every minute of the day and night. Oxygen, a gas found in air, is taken in by the respiratory system – the nose, windpipe, and lungs. As we breathe in, oxygen enters the lungs and passes into the blood. A waste gas, carbon dioxide, passes from the blood into the lungs and is removed when we breathe out.

Air flows through the nasal cavity

Air is breathed in through the nose and mouth

HOW THE LUNGS WORK

Air is sucked into the lungs through the trachea, or windpipe, which splits into two narrow tubes called bronchi. The bronchi branch out into tiny tubes called bronchioles. At the end of these are air bags, called alveoli. Oxygen passes through the thin walls of the alveoli and into blood flowing through blood vessels.

Voice box is at the top of the windpipe

Air passes along the windpipe to the lungs

Bronchi

Bronchioles

Right lung has three lobes

Bronchiole

Blood vessel

Alveoli

Close-up of the inside of a lung

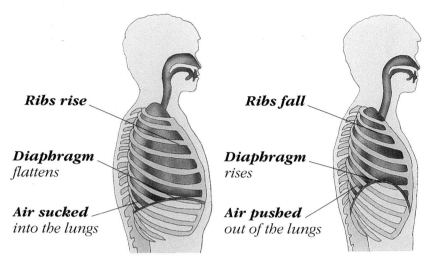

Ribs rise

Diaphragm *flattens*

Air sucked *into the lungs*

Breathing in

Ribs fall

Diaphragm *rises*

Air pushed *out of the lungs*

Breathing out

BREATHING IN AND OUT

Breathing depends on the movement of the ribs and a sheet of muscle, called the diaphragm, which lies below the lungs. To breathe in, the ribs rise and the diaphragm flattens. This makes space for the lungs to expand and suck in air. To breathe out, the ribs fall and the diaphragm rises to squeeze air out of the lungs.

MAKING SOUND

The voice box is at the top of the windpipe. Two flaps called vocal cords run across it. Normally they are open. When we speak, they close. Air flowing past the closed cords makes them vibrate and produce sounds.

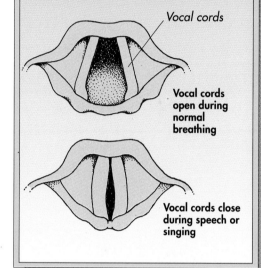

Vocal cords

Vocal cords open during normal breathing

Vocal cords close during speech or singing

Inside the lungs

Lobe

Left lung

AMAZING FACTS

★ The lungs have more than 300 million alveoli. Spread out flat, they would cover an area more than half the size of a tennis court.

★ Opera singers learn to control the movement of their diaphragms to make their voices strong.

FIND OUT MORE
DANCE, DRAMA, AND MUSIC: Singing
PLANT LIFE: Respiration

Blood Circulation

Blood is the body's delivery and removal system. It keeps cells alive by delivering food and oxygen to them and by removing their unwanted wastes. It also protects the body from illness by destroying germs, and helps to keep the body warm. Blood is pumped around the body by the heart along tubes called blood vessels. There are three types – arteries, capillaries, and veins.

Red blood cells
carry oxygen to the body's tissues

Plasma is
the liquid part of blood

Contents of the blood inside an artery

Platelets help
the blood clot to seal any leaks

White blood cells
help to fight disease

Arteries have strong
walls so they do not burst as blood is pumped through them by the heart

AMAZING FACTS

★ About 2 million new red blood cells are made in bone marrow every second.

★ A single drop of blood contains about 250 million cells.

INSIDE BLOOD

Blood has two main parts – plasma and blood cells. Plasma is the liquid part of blood. It delivers dissolved food to all the body's cells and removes their wastes. Billions of blood cells – mostly red blood cells, with white blood cells and platelets – float in the plasma.

It only needs a very light touch to feel the pulse in your wrist

TAKING A PULSE

Each time the heart beats, it sends a surge of blood along an artery. This is called a pulse. You can feel your own pulse on the inside of your wrist. Measure your pulse rate by counting the number of beats you feel with your fingertips in one minute. Most people's pulse rate when they are resting is between 60 and 80 beats a minute.

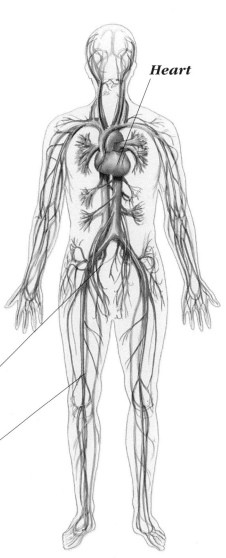

Heart

Arteries (in red)
carry oxygen-rich blood to all parts of the body

Veins (in blue)
carry blood low in oxygen from the body to the heart

Veins and arteries in the body

BLOOD CELLS

Disk-shaped red blood cells carry oxygen from the lungs to all body cells. White blood cells defend the body from infection by destroying germs. Platelets are the smallest cells. They help the blood to clot, or thicken, to block small leaks in blood vessels and stop bleeding.

Magnified red blood cells

BLOOD FLOW

The heart pumps oxygen-rich blood to all parts of the body along arteries. Arteries branch to form capillaries that deliver oxygen to the body's cells, and then join to form veins. Veins carry oxygen-poor blood back to the heart. It is then pumped to the lungs where it picks up more oxygen.

FIND OUT MORE
GREAT LIVES: William Harvey
REPTILES AND AMPHIBIANS: Blood

The Heart

The heart is a hollow muscular pump that pushes blood around the body. It lies inside the chest, slightly to the left-hand side. A wall divides the heart into left and right sides. Each side has two chambers – the upper atrium and the lower ventricle. The lower ventricle has a thicker muscle wall than the upper atrium. Major blood vessels carry blood into each atrium and out of each ventricle.

AMAZING FACTS

★ In an average lifetime, the human heart beats over 3 billion times without stopping.

★ Every day, the heart pumps enough blood to fill a 15,000-liter (4,000-gallon) tanker.

INSIDE THE HEART

The left atrium receives oxygen-rich blood from the lungs, which the left ventricle pumps to the body along an artery called the aorta. Oxygen-poor blood returns to the right atrium through the vena cava and is pumped to the lungs, to pick up oxygen, along the pulmonary artery.

Upper vena cava *returns oxygen-poor blood from the upper body to the heart*

Aorta carries *oxygen-rich blood from the heart to the body*

Cross-section of the heart

Right atrium *receives blood from the vena cava*

Valves stop blood *from flowing in the wrong direction*

Right ventricle *receives blood from the right atrium and pumps it to the lungs via the pulmonary artery*

Lower vena cava *returns oxygen-poor blood from the lower body to the right atrium*

THE HEARTBEAT

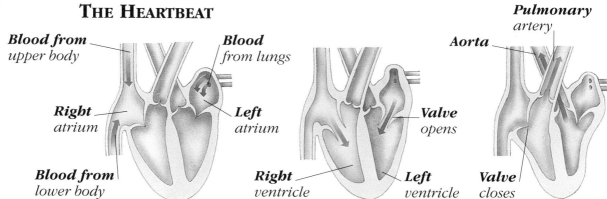

Blood from upper body

Blood from lungs

Right atrium

Left atrium

Blood from lower body

Right ventricle

Valve opens

Left ventricle

Pulmonary artery

Aorta

Valve closes

1 **Blood flows from** the body into the right atrium and from the lungs into the left atrium.

2 **The muscles in the** atrium walls squeeze in, forcing the blood down into the ventricles.

3 **The ventricle walls** contract, and the blood is squeezed upward into the arteries.

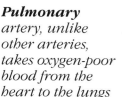

Pulmonary artery, unlike other arteries, takes oxygen-poor blood from the heart to the lungs

Pulmonary veins, unlike other veins, carry oxygen-rich blood from the lungs to the heart

Left atrium receives blood from the pulmonary veins

Valve stops blood from flowing backward into the atrium

Left ventricle receives blood from the left atrium and pumps it to the body via the aorta

Heart wall is made of muscle

LISTENING TO THE HEART

Each time the heart beats, it produces sounds. These sounds are caused by heart valves slamming shut. You can hear heart sounds by putting your ear to someone's chest or by listening through an instrument called a stethoscope.

A stethoscope amplifies, or makes louder, the heart's sounds

FIND OUT MORE
GREAT INVENTIONS: Stethoscope
INSIDE MACHINES: Valves

Keeping Fit

The heart is a muscle, so with regular exercise it becomes better at supplying the body with oxygen. Exercise helps all our other muscles become stronger, too, and keeps us fit.

During aerobic exercise, such as running, the heart beats faster and the lungs work harder. This is because the muscles that move the body demand extra food and oxygen to give them energy. Aerobic exercise makes the heart and lungs stronger and better at doing their job. Other types of exercise, such as yoga, improve fitness by strengthening muscles and keeping the body flexible.

Jumping rope is a type of aerobic exercise

HIGH-INTENSITY EXERCISE

Jumping rope, bicycling, roller-blading, and running are good ways to improve stamina. Improved stamina means the body can exercise for longer periods because the heart is better at supplying oxygen and food to the muscles.

Safety helmet *is an important piece of protective equipment*

Arm pads keep *wrists and elbows protected*

Legs and arms *work hard together to maintain balance and speed*

Protective knee pads *help prevent injury*

Boots *should fit comfortably*

Roller-blading increases the heart rate

One of the basic yoga positions

STRETCH AND RELAX

In yoga, the body and mind work together. A variety of positions, called postures, stretch the muscles. Breathing exercises slow down the heartbeat to give a state of relaxation.

WALKING FOR FITNESS

Gentle exercise is much better than none at all. Walking is a good way to start getting healthier. Regular walking, instead of riding in a bus or car, will improve fitness levels, and the heart will steadily become stronger and fitter.

Walking helps to keep you fit

RUNNERS

Running is a demanding sport. Sprinters need powerful leg muscles to produce a sudden burst of speed over short distances. Long-distance runners need stamina and energy reserves to keep them going.

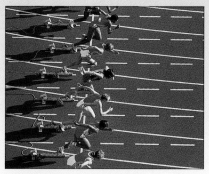

Sprinters racing away from the starting blocks

Swimming is good all-round exercise

SINK OR SWIM

Swimming provides good exercise. It uses all the important muscles in the body. There is no strain on any of the joints because the water supports the weight of the body. Swimming also encourages strong, regular breathing.

FIND OUT MORE
GREAT LIVES: Sporting stars
SPORT: Swimming

Digestive System

The body needs food to give it energy, to make it grow, and to repair itself. The food we eat is made up of complex substances called nutrients. These complex nutrients have to be broken down into simpler parts so the body can use them. That is the job of the digestive system. Simple nutrients pass into the blood and are carried to all the body's cells.

A LONG JOURNEY

After swallowing, food is squeezed down the esophagus into the stomach, where it is churned up into a paste. This enters the small intestine, where most digestion happens and simple nutrients pass into the blood. Any waste enters the large intestine and is stored in the rectum before leaving the body.

Parts of the digestive system

Esophagus

Liver

Small intestine
where digestion takes place

Large intestine
absorbs water from waste

Rectum

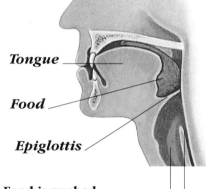

Tongue

Food

Epiglottis

Food is pushed to the back of the mouth by the tongue

Esophagus

Windpipe

Food

Esophagus

Epiglottis

Windpipe

Epiglottis closes the windpipe to stop food from entering the lungs

SWALLOWING FOOD

The first part of digestion happens inside the mouth. Food is cut and crushed by the teeth, and mixed with slimy saliva into a soft pulp by the tongue. When the tongue pushes chewed food into the throat, it is automatically swallowed and passes into the esophagus.

INSIDE THE STOMACH

The walls of the stomach stretch to make room for food when it arrives. The stomach's lining releases an acidic juice. This mixes with the food, starts to digest it, and kills any germs. The muscular walls contract and churn up the food and juice into a soupy paste. As the body becomes busy digesting food, especially after a big meal, a person may feel sleepy.

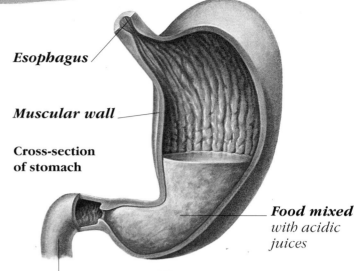

Esophagus

Muscular wall

Cross-section of stomach

Food mixed with acidic juices

Small intestine

AMAZING FACTS

★ If stretched out, an adult's intestines would be nearly 7 m (23 ft) long.

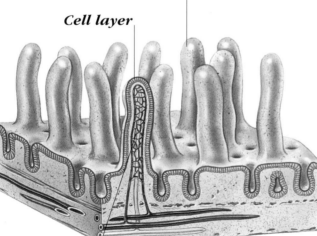

Stomach churns food into a thick paste

Villi

Cell layer

Blood flowing through capillaries picks up digested food

Cross-section of small intestine showing villi

FOOD PROCESSING

Most digestion takes place as food passes along the small intestine. Its lining is covered with circular folds. On these folds are tiny fingerlike villi. Digested food passes through the walls of the villi and into blood capillaries. The blood then carries the digested food to where it is needed in the body.

FIND OUT MORE
BIRDS: Saliva
INSECTS AND SPIDERS: Feeding

Clearing Waste

The body's cells are like tiny chemical factories. They need food, water, and oxygen to work and keep the body alive. As they work, cells produce wastes. These wastes are poisonous to the body and must be removed by special organs. Some wastes are filtered from the blood by the two kidneys to form urine. Others are made harmless by the liver. Carbon dioxide is breathed out through the lungs.

THE LUNGS
Inside every cell in the body, oxygen and food combine to release energy. This process also releases carbon dioxide as waste. Carbon dioxide is carried by the blood to the lungs and is breathed out.

Renal artery *carries blood into the kidneys*

Renal vein *carries blood out of the kidneys*

GETTING RID OF URINE
Urine is made in both of the kidneys and flows into a stretchy bag, the bladder, where it is stored. When the bladder is full, it sends messages to the brain. We then feel the need to go to the bathroom. Babies cannot choose when to release urine, so they need to wear a diaper.

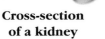

Millions of *nephrons are found in the outer part of the kidney*

Cross-section of a kidney

Ureter *carries urine to the bladder*

Waste-clearing organs

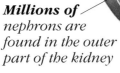

Baby wearing a diaper

INSIDE THE KIDNEYS
The kidneys receive a quarter of the blood pumped by the heart. Inside the kidneys millions of nephrons, tiny filters, remove waste and water from this blood to make urine. Cleaned blood leaves the kidney along the renal vein.

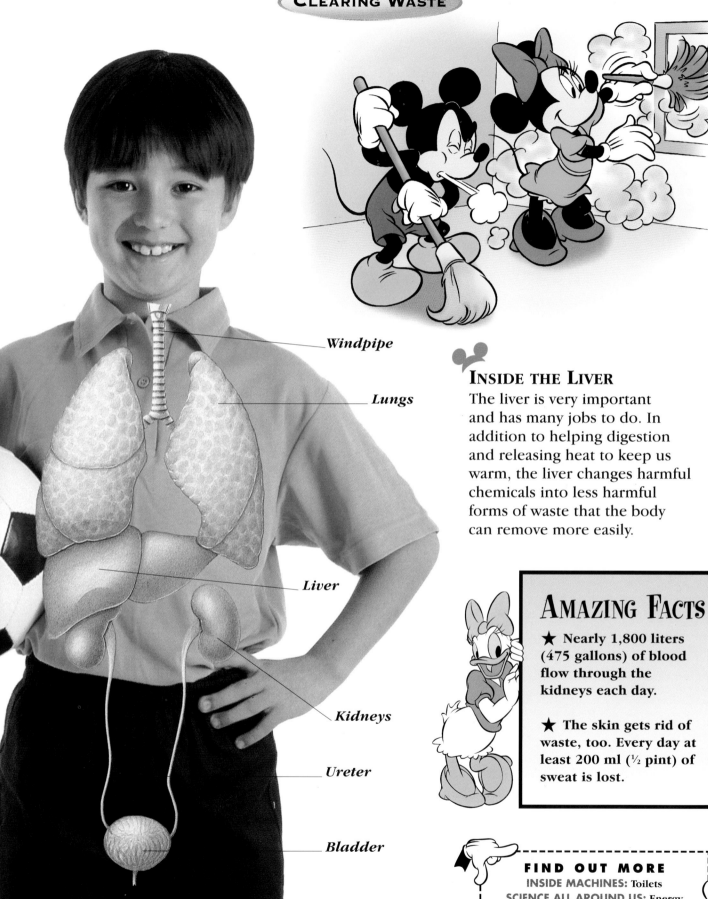

Windpipe

Lungs

Liver

Kidneys

Ureter

Bladder

INSIDE THE LIVER

The liver is very important and has many jobs to do. In addition to helping digestion and releasing heat to keep us warm, the liver changes harmful chemicals into less harmful forms of waste that the body can remove more easily.

AMAZING FACTS

★ Nearly 1,800 liters (475 gallons) of blood flow through the kidneys each day.

★ The skin gets rid of waste, too. Every day at least 200 ml (½ pint) of sweat is lost.

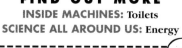

FIND OUT MORE
INSIDE MACHINES: Toilets
SCIENCE ALL AROUND US: Energy

Eating for Health

Food contains nutrients that give the body energy and make it grow. To keep healthy we need to eat a range of different nutrients.

Nutrients include carbohydrates, proteins, fats, vitamins, and minerals. Carbohydrates in starchy and sugary foods give us energy. Proteins are nutrients used for growth and repair. Fats provide energy and also help keep us warm. Vitamins and minerals, needed in small amounts, help keep the body healthy. The body also needs fiber, which is plant material that the body cannot digest. It helps keep the digestive system working properly.

A Wide Choice

Your diet is the food you eat every day. A balanced diet is one that supplies a mixture of nutrients to help your body stay healthy. Carbohydrates should form most of your diet, with proteins and fats eaten in smaller amounts. You should also eat plenty of fresh fruit and vegetables every day.

A balanced diet is important for health

Butter, cream, *cheese, milk, oils, and nuts have a high fat content*

Children need to drink about 1 liter (2 pints) of fluid every day

Meat, fish, eggs, *legumes, and seeds are high in protein*

Burger

French fries

Soft drink

Ice cream

Chocolate

Chips

These foods should only be eaten in small amounts

Cupcakes

BAG OF WATER

In total, water makes up about two-thirds of the body's weight. There is more water in the body than any other substance. Without water the body's cells cannot work, so it is important that we drink plenty of liquid throughout the day.

UNHEALTHY DIETS

Foods such as burgers, french fries, and chocolate contain a lot of fat. These foods can harm the body if eaten regularly in large amounts.

Whole-grain bread, rice, pasta, and flour are rich in carbohydrates and fiber

Fruit and vegetables contain vitamins and minerals as well as fiber

Most of the body's water is held inside the cells

CALORIES

The body uses the energy from food to carry out its daily activities. This energy is measured in calories. If we take in more calories than our body needs, we store the extra as fat and put on weight. If we take in too few, we lose weight.

FIND OUT MORE
CHILDREN OF THE WORLD: Markets
TRAVELERS AND EXPLORERS: Food

33

Brain Power

 The brain is the body's control center. Over 100 billion nerve cells are packed into this soft, wrinkled structure protected only by the skull. The nerve cells form a communication network across which messages flash at high speed every second. Our brain enables us to think and feel, it stores our memories, and it makes us move.

Cerebrum makes up
90 percent of the brain

Cerebellum
controls messages
sent to the muscles

Brain stem
joins the brain to
the spinal cord

Main parts
of the brain

Left side
deals with
scientific skills

Right side
deals with
creative skills

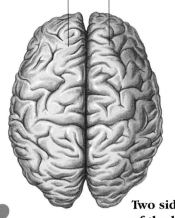

Two sides
of the brain

SIDE BY SIDE

The brain has two sides. The left side controls the right half of the body, and the right side controls the left half. Each side is also involved with different skills. The right side deals with music, art, and creative activities. The left side deals with speech, numbers, and problem solving.

PARTS OF THE BRAIN

The brain is divided into three main parts. The largest is the cerebrum, which deals with thinking, feeling, and doing. The cerebellum, at the back of the brain, makes sure the body balances and moves smoothly. The brain stem controls breathing and heart rate.

RESTFUL SLEEP

While we sleep, the body rests and repairs itself. The brain is still active, however, even during deep sleep. It sorts the previous day's events and stores memories.

Thin outer layer of the cerebrum is where information is processed

LEARNING A SKILL

It can take a long time to learn new skills, such as adding and subtracting or playing a musical instrument. Once learned, these skills are stored in the brain's memory bank. They can then be recalled when needed and do not have to be learned again.

Adding and subtracting with an abacus

Messages sent from the brain make the fingers move together to make the right notes

AMAZING FACTS

★ The brain uses one-fifth of the body's energy yet is just one-fiftieth of the body's weight.

★ There is no link between brain size and intelligence.

FIND OUT MORE
GREAT INVENTIONS: Computers
GREAT LIVES: Inventors

The Nervous System

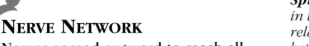 **E**very activity we carry out, from smelling a flower to climbing a ladder, depends on the nervous system, which has three parts. The brain, the control center, receives messages, sorts and stores them, and sends out instructions. A network of nerves relays information to and from all parts of the body. The spinal cord is a communication highway that links nerves to the brain.

NERVE NETWORK
Nerves spread outward to reach all parts of the body. Cranial nerves, from the brain, control our facial expressions and carry information from our eyes and ears to the brain. Spinal nerves, from the spinal cord, control our movements and carry information about touch.

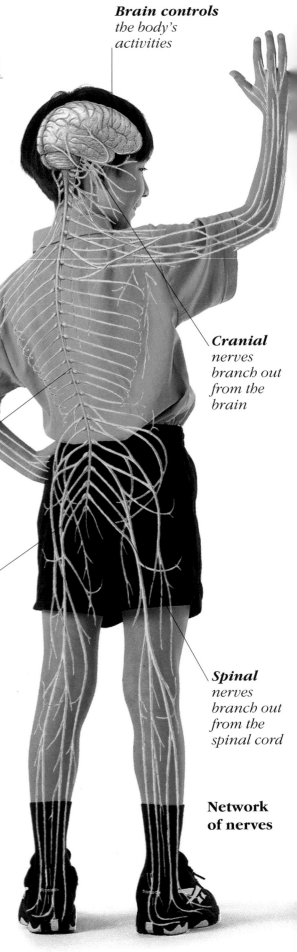

Brain controls the body's activities

Cranial nerves branch out from the brain

Spinal cord, in the backbone, relays messages between the body and brain

Sciatic nerve controls muscles in the leg and foot

Spinal nerves branch out from the spinal cord

Network of nerves

AMAZING FACTS
★ The body's thickest nerve, the sciatic nerve, is as wide as a child's middle finger. It runs from the spinal cord into each leg.

★ Most nerve messages pass along the spinal cord through the neck. This is why neck injuries can be serious and may cause paralysis, or a loss of movement.

INSIDE NERVES

Nerves are made up of bundles of very long, thin nerve cells called neurons. Sensory neurons carry messages to the brain from sensors in the eyes, ears, tongue, nose, and skin. These allow us to sense things. Motor neurons carry instructions from the brain to muscles to make them move.

Sensory neurons carry messages that enable us to smell

Carrying out a task uses sensory and motor neurons

FAST REFLEXES

Reflex actions work quickly to protect us from danger. If we step on a pin, sensors in the skin of the foot send messages to the spinal cord. This sends instructions directly to the leg muscles to pull the foot away. The brain does not receive the message to feel pain until the reflex has taken place.

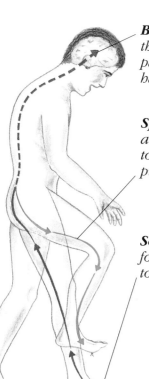

Brain receives the message to feel pain after the foot has been pulled away

Spinal cord sends a message straight to the muscles to pull the foot away

Sensors in the foot send a message to the spinal cord

Pin

Reflex action

A reflex action makes the eyes blink

Blinking is a reflex action

GOOD REFLEXES

A sudden movement near the face makes the eyes blink. This reflex action helps protect the eyes from harm. Tapping below the knee with a small hammer should make the leg kick upward. Doctors test this reflex to make sure the nervous system is working properly.

FIND OUT MORE
GREAT INVENTIONS: Anesthetic
GREAT LIVES: Hua Tuo

Sight and Touch

The eyes and skin are sensory organs. They keep the brain updated with information about what is happening around the body. Both contain millions of tiny sensors that send messages along nerves to the brain. Sensors in the eyes respond to light and, through the brain, let us see the world. Sensors in the skin respond to touch and allow us to feel.

BRIGHT EYES

In order for us to see, the right amount of light must enter the eye. In dim light, the pupil widens to let more light in. In bright light, the pupil gets smaller so that the retina is not damaged.

Pupil expands in dim light to let in more light

Normal size of pupil

Pupil shrinks in bright light to protect the retina

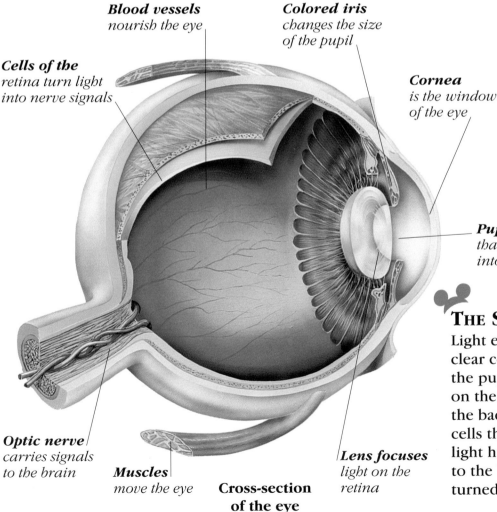

Blood vessels *nourish the eye*

Colored iris *changes the size of the pupil*

Cells of the *retina turn light into nerve signals*

Cornea *is the window of the eye*

Pupil is a hole *that lets light into the eye*

Optic nerve *carries signals to the brain*

Muscles *move the eye*

Cross-section of the eye

Lens focuses *light on the retina*

THE SEEING EYE

Light enters the eye through the clear cornea. It then passes through the pupil and is focused by the lens on the retina. This thin layer covers the back of the eye and contains cells that are sensitive to light. When light hits the cells, they send signals to the brain. There, the signals are turned into pictures so we can see.

CLEANING THE EYE

Tears are constantly released by tear-producing glands above each eye. They wash over the eyes each time you blink. Tears remove dust, kill germs, and keep the cornea moist. They empty through the tear ducts, into the nose. If you cry, tears spill onto your cheeks and you also get a runny nose.

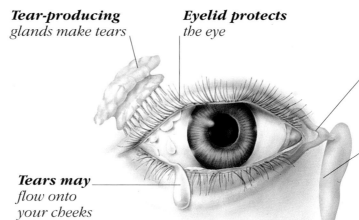

Tear-producing *glands make tears*

Eyelid protects *the eye*

Tear duct *drains away tears into the nose*

Duct carries *tears to the inside of the nose*

Tears may *flow onto your cheeks*

Keeping the eye clean

Tears gather *inside your nose, and may make it run*

AMAZING FACTS

★ The human eye contains 70 percent of the body's sensors.

SENSE OF TOUCH

Millions of tiny sensors lie just below the skin's surface. Some detect light touch, some firm pressure, and others pain, heat, and cold. When you touch something, these sensors send signals to the brain. These signals tell you if something is rough or smooth, hard or soft, hot or cold, or ticklish. The most sensitive parts of the body, with most sensors, are the eyes, tongue, lips, fingers, feet, and toes.

Flame feels *dangerously hot, so you keep your hands well away*

Ice cubes feel *hard, cold, and wet*

Cat's fur feels *soft and warm*

FIND OUT MORE
INSIDE MACHINES: Sensors
SCIENCE ALL AROUND US: Eyes

Smell and Taste

The senses of smell and taste are closely linked. Both detect chemicals. Smell sensors are found at the top of the nasal cavity behind the nose. They detect chemicals in the air. Taste sensors are found on the tongue. They detect chemicals in food and drink. Together, our senses of smell and taste enable us to enjoy the flavors of food and to avoid things that may be harmful.

SENSING SMELLS

Smell sensors in the nasal cavity detect odor particles in air that is breathed in. These odors come from substances such as food, perfume, or smoke. The sensors send signals to the brain, which identifies the smell.

Brain interprets signals from the nose and tongue

Messages about smell are sent along the olfactory nerves to the brain

Olfactory nerves are smell sensors

Nasal cavity

Tongue

Nerves carry taste messages to the brain

AMAZING FACTS

★ Most people can tell the difference between 10,000 different odors.

★ Your sense of smell is 10,000 times keener than your sense of taste.

Detecting smell and taste

TASTE SENSATIONS

Tiny clusters of cells called taste buds are scattered all over the tongue. Groups of taste buds in different areas respond to the four main taste sensations: bitter, salty, sour, and sweet. Nerve fibers in the taste buds carry messages to the brain, enabling you to taste.

Tasting and enjoying food

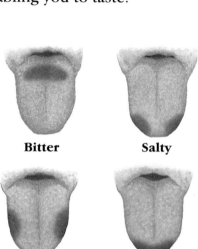

Bitter

Salty

Sour

Sweet

ENJOYING FOOD

Our senses of taste and smell work together. The sense of smell is much more sensitive than the sense of taste. If you have a bad cold and your nose is blocked, food tastes bland and lacks flavor. If you cover your nose, you probably won't be able to taste what you are eating.

Papillae
in two sizes

**Microscopic view
of the tongue**

TASTE BUDS

The surface of the tongue is covered with thousands of tiny bumps, called papillae. The taste buds lie at the base and on the sides of the papillae.

FIND OUT MORE
MAMMALS: Skunk
TRAVELERS AND EXPLORERS: Spicy foods

Hearing and Balance

Our ears enable us to hear sounds. Sound travels as waves of vibrations, tiny movements of the air. Inside the ear, these vibrations stimulate sensors that send signals to the brain. In the brain, the signals are translated back into words, music, or other sounds. The ears also help the body to balance.

INSIDE THE EAR

Sounds entering the ear canal make the eardrum shake. The vibration passes along three bones, called the ossicles, and into the cochlea. Here, a fluid starts to ripple and bends tiny hairs that send a signal along nerve fibers to the brain.

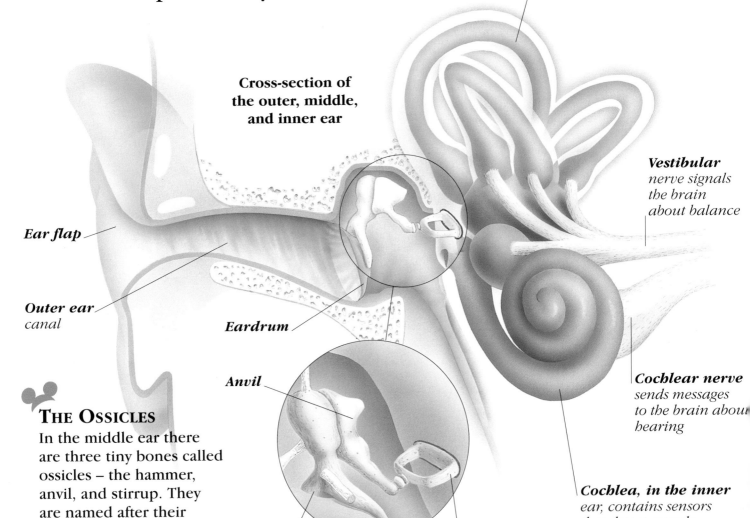

Semicircular canals *in the inner ear detect movements of the head*

Cross-section of the outer, middle, and inner ear

Ear flap

Outer ear *canal*

Eardrum

Vestibular *nerve signals the brain about balance*

Cochlear nerve *sends messages to the brain about hearing*

Cochlea, in the inner *ear, contains sensors that detect sounds*

Anvil

THE OSSICLES

In the middle ear there are three tiny bones called ossicles – the hammer, anvil, and stirrup. They are named after their shapes. These bones pass vibrations from the eardrum to the inner ear.

Hammer

Ossicles in the middle ear

Stirrup is *the innermost ossicle*

LOUD AND SOFT

The loudness of different sounds is measured in decibels (dB). A whisper measures about 20 decibels, while a firework measures about 100. Sounds greater than 130 decibels are painful to the human ear.

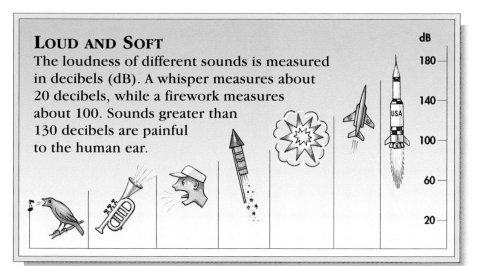

dB
180
140
100
60
20

USA

AMAZING FACTS

★ Cats and bats can hear extremely high-pitched sounds that the human ear is unable to detect.

★ The stirrup, the smallest bone in the body, is just 3 mm (⅛ in) long.

BALANCING ACT

Our ears help us to balance. Inside each ear there are three semicircular canals filled with fluid. As the head moves, the fluid moves and sensors send signals to the brain about the changing position of the head. The brain then sends instructions to make sure the body is still balanced.

Semicircular canals tell your brain which way up your body is, so that you can balance

ANIMAL EARS

Some animals, such as the rabbit or the fox, have large ear flaps, which they can move toward sounds. The ear flaps help the animals to pick up quiet sounds and to pinpoint where they are coming from. This is useful when they are looking for food or avoiding enemies.

Rabbit

FIND OUT MORE
MAMMALS: Bats
SCIENCE ALL AROUND US: Sound

A New Life

A new life begins when an egg from a woman and a sperm from a man join together to make a fertilized egg. Together, the sperm and egg contain the information needed to make a new person. The fertilized egg divides over and over again and grows into a baby inside the woman's body.

FERTILIZING THE EGG

After sperm enter a woman's body, they swim along the Fallopian tubes. If an egg is in the tube, the sperm surround it. A single sperm then breaks through the egg's outer barrier and fertilizes the egg. The fertilized egg divides, and a ball of cells called an embryo arrives in the uterus.

One sperm fertilizes the egg when the two join together

Many sperm try to enter the egg

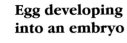

Egg developing into an embryo

INSIDE A MAN

Sperm are produced inside a man's testes. The two testes hang inside a bag of skin called the scrotum. The sperm travel from the testes along tiny tubes, and leave the body through the penis.

Sperm travel to the penis through tiny tubes

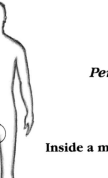

Penis

Inside a man

Testes make sperm cells

|Scrotum

AMAZING FACTS

★ Millions of sperm are made in a man's testes every day.

★ A girl is born with all the eggs she will ever have. Her tiny ovaries contain more than 2 million eggs.

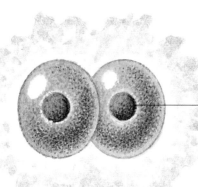

After 36 hours *the fertilized egg divides into two cells*

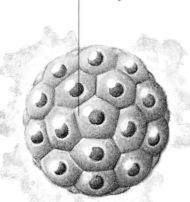

The embryo, a *tiny ball of cells, plants itself in the wall of the uterus*

Identical twins

TWINS

Sometimes when a fertilized egg divides, the two cells separate. These two cells contain the same information and will develop into identical twins. Fraternal, or non-identical, twins are produced when two eggs are released from the ovaries and both are fertilized at the same time.

INSIDE A WOMAN

A woman's eggs are stored inside her ovaries and a single one is released every month. An egg travels slowly from the ovary along a Fallopian tube. If it meets a sperm, it may be fertilized. A fertilized egg takes about six days to reach the uterus, where it grows into a baby.

Fallopian tube *collects the egg from the ovary*

Fallopian tube is *where the egg meets the sperm*

Embryo plants *itself in the lining of the uterus*

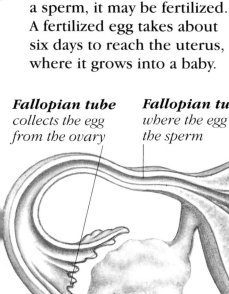

Ovary is where *eggs are kept*

Uterus, *or womb*

Cervix is the *entrance to the uterus*

Vagina

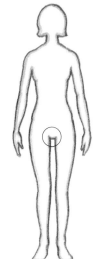

Inside a woman

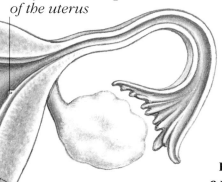

FIND OUT MORE
INSECTS AND SPIDERS: Eggs
PLANT LIFE: Fertilization

Baby in Waiting

It takes nine months for a fertilized egg to grow into a fully developed baby. During this period the egg divides many times to produce the many billions of cells needed to make a human. At first it is called an embryo, but after eight weeks in the uterus the growing baby is called a fetus. The fetus is attached to its mother by the placenta. This provides it with food and oxygen.

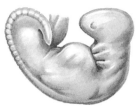

At five weeks the tiny baby is called an embryo and it has the beginnings of most body systems

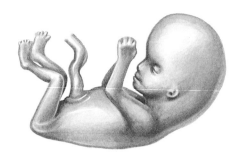

At nine weeks all the main parts of the fetus's body have been made

GETTING BIGGER

The cells of the fetus divide rapidly. Groups of cells develop into different body parts, such as the heart, lungs, brain, hands, and feet. At eight weeks old, the fetus looks human, although it is only 2.5 cm (1 in) long. After 38 weeks (nine months), the fetus is ready to be born.

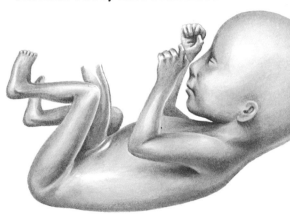

At 13 weeks the limbs are growing faster than the rest of body

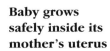

Baby grows safely inside its mother's uterus

AMAZING FACTS

★ A woman's uterus will stretch up to 20 times its normal size during pregnancy.

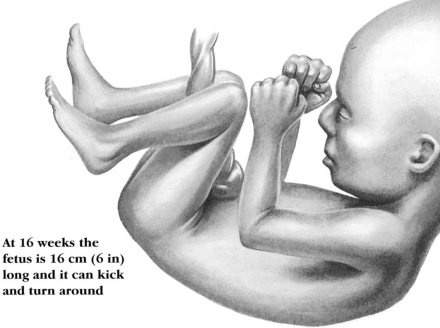

At 16 weeks the fetus is 16 cm (6 in) long and it can kick and turn around

CORD CONNECTION

The placenta is attached to the wall of the uterus. Food and oxygen pass from the mother's blood across the placenta and into the fetus along a tube called the umbilical cord. After birth, the umbilical cord is cut, leaving a small dimple on the baby's abdomen called the navel.

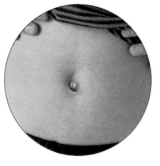

Navel on the abdomen

NEWBORN BABY

A baby takes its first breath into its lungs as soon as it is born. As its umbilical cord is cut, the baby is separated from its mother's body and it begins life on its own.

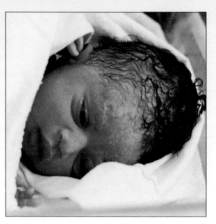

Newborn baby

By 38 weeks the baby is positioned head down, ready to be born

Umbilical cord

Placenta

Amniotic fluid, a watery liquid, surrounds and protects the baby

READY FOR BIRTH

When a baby is ready to be born, the muscular walls of the mother's uterus push it out through the cervix and vagina. Most babies are born head first. The placenta slips out of the mother's body a few minutes later.

Uterus

Cervix opens so the baby can be pushed out

Muscular walls of the uterus

Vagina

Baby ready to be born

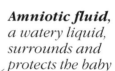

FIND OUT MORE
BIRDS: Young
REPTILES AND AMPHIBIANS: Eggs

Growing Up

Everyone's body follows the same pattern of changes through life. When a baby is born, it can cry for milk and suck at its mother's breast, but is totally helpless. A baby grows quickly in the first two years and steadily through childhood as it learns to walk, talk, and perform other skills. Between 10 and 15 years of age, boys and girls grow rapidly and become adults.

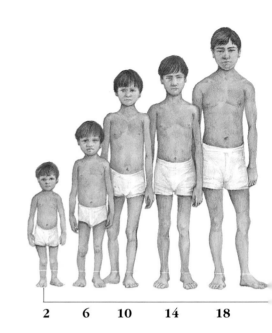

2   6   10   14   18

LEARNING TO WALK

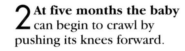

2 At five months the baby can begin to crawl by pushing its knees forward.

1 Between one and two months a baby can lift up its head while lying on its tummy.

3 At 10 months most babies can crawl easily, although some shuffle along on their bottoms instead.

4 At one year, with a little help, a baby can pull itself up into a standing position.

5 By about 14 months most children can walk without help.

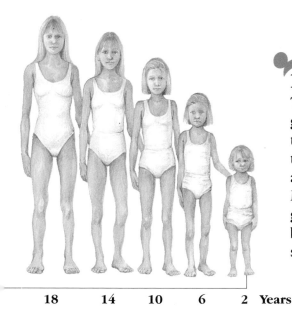

BODY CHANGES

The body changes as it grows. On average, at the age of 11 girls begin to change into women, and at 13, boys into men. Most people are fully grown by the age of 20, but everyone grows at slightly different rates.

| 18 | 14 | 10 | 6 | 2 | Years |

How your body changes as you grow

GROWTH HORMONES

The speed at which the body grows is controlled by chemical substances called hormones. They are made in body parts called glands. Hormones are released straight into the bloodstream.

Three generations of one family

GROWING OLDER

The body changes less during its adult years. After the age of about 40, the skin begins to wrinkle and sometimes the hair turns gray. Taking care of the body helps people to stay healthy well into old age.

AMAZING FACTS

★ At age seven, a girl is three-quarters her adult height; a boy reaches this stage at age nine.

★ On average, Japanese people live longer than anyone else in the world.

FIND OUT MORE
INSECTS AND SPIDERS: Metamorphosis
MAMMALS: Mammary glands

Being Yourself

People in the same family often look like each other and behave in similar ways. Yet no two people are exactly the same. Everyone is an individual with his or her own personality.

Some parts of our personality are inherited from our parents. Every child inherits a different combination of characteristics that make up their personality, so even brothers and sisters are different from each other. Other parts of our personality develop from our experiences of life. These are stored in our memory and affect how we think, feel, and behave.

Children can learn skills and hobbies from their parents

ALL SORTS OF PEOPLE

People are different not just because of the way they look but because of the way they think, behave, and express themselves. Sometimes it is possible to learn about someone's personality by looking at the expressions on their face.

Happiness

Confidence

Moodiness

Expressing feelings

Studiousness

Shyness

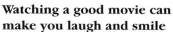
Watching a good movie can make you laugh and smile

HAVING FEELINGS

Feelings are powerful. Smiles or tears are the outward signs of our inner emotions. These are affected not only by people and events but also by pictures, music, plays, books, and movies.

Family vacation photo

CHILDHOOD MEMORIES

Childhood experiences and upbringing can affect a person's personality. Both good and bad memories are stored in the brain. Sometimes a little reminder, such as a vacation photograph, can bring back powerful stored-up feelings.

FIND OUT MORE
COMMUNICATIONS: Body language
PLANT LIFE: Genetics

Defending the Body

The body is under constant attack from germs, such as bacteria and viruses, that cause diseases. A healthy body has several ways of defending itself. Cuts in the skin close up to stop germs from entering. White blood cells either eat germs or release chemicals called antibodies to destroy them.

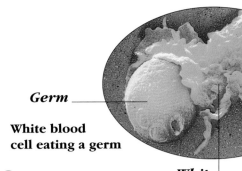

Germs

White blood cell eating a germ

White blood cell

ON THE ATTACK

Some white blood cells "remember" the identity of any invading bacteria or viruses. If these germs reappear, these cells immediately release killer chemicals called antibodies to destroy them. Other white blood cells hunt germs and destroy them by eating them.

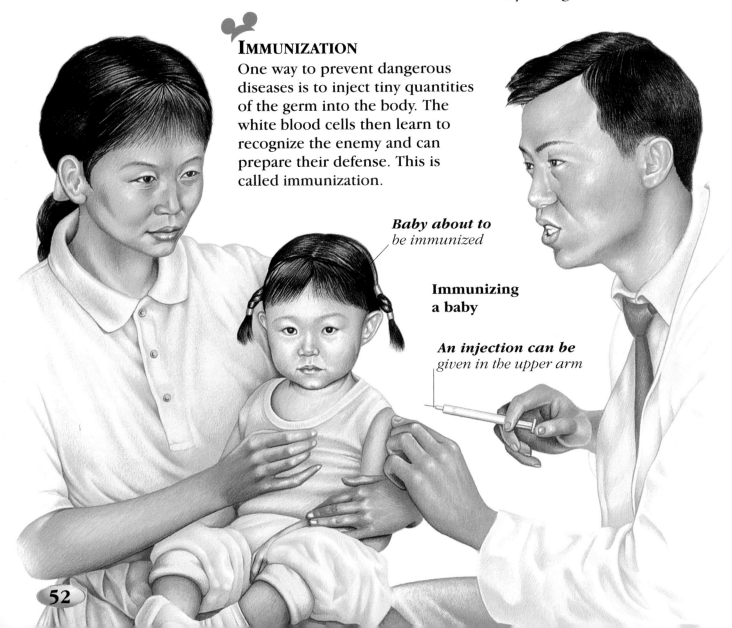

IMMUNIZATION

One way to prevent dangerous diseases is to inject tiny quantities of the germ into the body. The white blood cells then learn to recognize the enemy and can prepare their defense. This is called immunization.

Baby about to be immunized

Immunizing a baby

An injection can be given in the upper arm

BROKEN BONES

Many parts of the body can heal themselves. A broken bone mends if the two ends are held together. First, blood clots at the break. Then repair tissue forms around the break. Finally, cells produce a bendy material called cartilage, which is eventually replaced by bone.

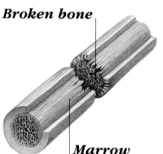

Broken bone

Marrow

Mending a broken bone

Blood clots *inside the break*

Repair tissue *forms around the break*

New cartilage *forms and will be replaced by bone*

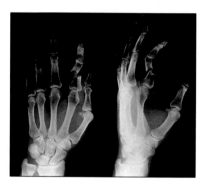

Broken finger revealed in an X-ray

AMAZING FACTS

★ Viruses are so small that billions of them could cover a pinhead.

★ Bacteria can divide once every 20 minutes.

High fever 39°C (102°F)

Mild fever 37.8°C (100°F)

Normal body temperature 37°C (98.6°F)

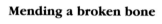

Temperature *is shown by the level of a liquid against a scale*

Thermometer

BODY TEMPERATURE

A rise above normal body temperature is called a fever. This is usually caused by germs invading the body. A mild fever can speed up the body's defenses and help to fight off disease. The body's temperature is usually taken in the mouth with an instrument called a thermometer.

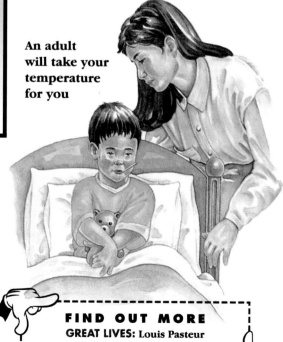

An adult will take your temperature for you

FIND OUT MORE
GREAT LIVES: Louis Pasteur
INSIDE MACHINES: X-rays

Helping Hands

Doctors and healers work in different ways to mend the body and cure disease. To do their work, they need to understand the body and the way that it functions.

It takes many years of study and research for scientists to produce medicines to fight a disease. In hospitals, surgeons are always trying new operations and methods of surgery. Today, patients can have their kidneys, lungs, or heart replaced if they are not working properly. Healers offer traditional forms of treatment, such as acupuncture, herbalism, reflexology, and massage therapy.

Different types of medicines

HEALING WITH NEEDLES

Acupuncture has been used in China for more than 3,500 years. It is based on the belief that the body flows with an energy called *chi*, which must be kept in balance to maintain good health. Thin needles are pushed a short way into the skin at special points on the body. Acupuncture is used to treat a variety of illnesses.

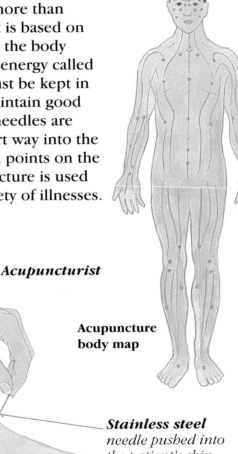

Acupuncturist

Acupuncture body map

Stainless steel *needle pushed into the patient's skin*

Treating a patient with acupuncture

HAVING AN OPERATION

Doctors sometimes have to cut into the body to treat an illness or injury. This is known as surgery. Operations are done in specially equipped operating rooms. Everything in the room is kept extremely clean to prevent infection.

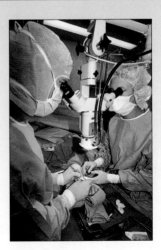

Surgical operation

COMFORTING TOUCH

Massage gives a feeling of wellbeing and eases stiffness that can be caused by tension and stress. Body massage using special oils is called aromatherapy. This uses the influence of smell to ease health problems. Reflexology is a special massage of the feet that is used to treat the whole body.

Hands massage
the skin very gently

Massaging a baby

HERBAL MEDICINE

People have known for centuries that plants can be used to treat illness. Herbalists understand the uses of different plants and mix them together to make medicines.

Herbal medicines

FIND OUT MORE
GREAT INVENTIONS: Antiseptics
PLANT LIFE: Medicines

Glossary of Key Words

Artery: A blood vessel that carries blood away from the heart to the rest of the body.

Blood: Liquid pumped along tubes called blood vessels by the heart. Blood transports food and oxygen to the body's cells, and helps defend the body from germs.

Bone marrow: The jellylike material found inside bones.

Brain: The control center of the nervous system that regulates many body activities, and helps a person to feel, think, and move.

Capillary: The smallest type of blood vessel. Capillaries link arteries and veins, and carry blood to and from all the body's cells.

Carbohydrates: A group of nutrients that supply the body with energy. Foods such as rice and potatoes are rich in carbohydrates.

Cell: The tiny structure that is the basic building block for all life. Many millions of cells make up the different parts of the human body.

Diaphragm: The sheet of muscle that separates the chest from the abdomen, and that plays an important part in breathing.

Digestion: The process by which food that is eaten is broken down into useful nutrients by fluids in the stomach and intestine.

Esophagus: The top part of the passage that takes food from the mouth down to the stomach.

Fats: A group of nutrients that provide energy and are stored under the skin to help keep the body warm.

Fertilized egg: An egg that has been joined by a sperm so that it can develop into an embryo.

Heart: The muscular organ, found in the chest, that pumps blood along blood vessels.

Intestine: The long tube in the body that digests and absorbs food from the stomach.

Joint: The place where two or more bones meet in the body. Most joints are flexible and enable the body to move.

Kidney: One of two organs, found just below the diaphragm, that remove waste and water from the blood to produce urine.

Liver: The large organ, just below the diaphragm, that stores food, cleans the blood, and helps keep the body warm.

Lung: One of two spongy organs found in the chest through which oxygen from air passes into the bloodstream.

Minerals: Simple substances, such as calcium and iron, that the body needs to stay alive and healthy.

Muscle: A stringy tissue that can be tightened or relaxed in order to move a part of the body.

Nerve: A long, thin structure that carries signals between the body, brain, and spinal cord.

Nutrients: Substances that are found in food which, after digestion, can be used by the body to build and repair cells.

Organ: An important part of the body, such as the heart or ear, that carries out a specific job or jobs.

Oxygen: A gas found in the air that is breathed in and used by cells to release energy from food.

Proteins: A group of nutrients used by the body for cell growth and repair. Foods rich in proteins include meat, fish, and beans.

Rectum: The last section of the intestine. Waste is stored here before it leaves the body as feces.

Sensors: The tiny cells found mainly in the eyes, ears, skin, nose, and tongue, which act as detectors telling the brain what is happening both inside and outside the body.

Skeleton: The bony frame that supports and protects the body.

Sperm: Tiny, tadpolelike cells that are produced by a man's testes. Sperm swim toward an egg to fertilize it and produce a baby.

Spinal cord: The bundle of nerves that runs down the neck and back, and which links the brain to the rest of the body.

Stomach: A muscular bag inside the body where food goes through its first main stage of digestion.

Structure: The way that parts of the body, for example, are put together or organized.

System: A group of organs that work together to carry out a particular job. The heart, blood, and blood vessels, for example, form the circulatory system, which carries blood around the body.

Tendon: The strong ropelike structure that attaches a muscle to a bone.

Uterus: The female organ in which a baby can develop.

Vein: A blood vessel that carries blood toward the heart from the rest of the body.

Vitamins: A group of nutrients, such as vitamins A, C, and D, needed to make sure the body works properly.

Index